Psychology and Health Series:

Volume 2

DEPRESSION

&

SADNESS

*NEVER LOSE HOPE: EVEN IF YOU
CAN'T SEE ANY*

Marios Savva

I dedicate all my books in my Psychology and Health series, to my loving family.

TABLE OF CONTENTS

THE AUTHOR

As an experienced psychologist currently living in Birmingham, England, and a member of the British Psychological Society, I now have the fervent desire to start writing books on psychology for people to read. I have endeavoured to make my books interesting to read and, with a little humour, as some psychology material can get 'heavy' and slightly complicated. DEPRESSION AND SADNESS: *NEVER LOSE HOPE - EVEN IF YOU CAN'T SEE ANY*, is the second book in the Psychology and Health series. Readers can contact me on: marios.spurs@hotmail.co.uk.

Other books by the author

Stress

Body Image

Know Thyself

Drugs and Addictions

I Want To Sleep

The Definition of Depression

Depression has been described as the "common cold" of psychological problems, affecting more than 10% of adults at any one time. People with major depression may experience a downcast mood and lose interest or pleasure in activities they might otherwise enjoy. They complain of feeling "down in the dumps" or have a sense of hopelessness about the future. They may have difficulty concentrating or summoning the energy to get going in the morning or even to get out of bed. They may experience changes in appetite (eating too much or too little) and sleep (sleeping either too much or too little or having difficulty getting back to sleep following early morning awakenings). They may be tearful at times and even contemplate or attempt suicide. In extreme cases, they may experience psychotic behaviours, such as hallucinations and delusions, such as believing that their body is rotting away.

Bereavement is useful (mourning the loss of a loved one is a natural adjustment); full-blown depression is not. Among the dreadful manifestations of major depression is self-hatred, a sense of worthlessness, joylessness, gloom, a sense of dread and alienation and above all, a stifling anxiety. Then there are the intellectual marks: confusion, failure of mental focus and lapse of memories, and, at a later stage, the mind becomes dominated by anarchic distortions and a sense that one's thoughts are engulfed by a tide of melancholy that destroys any enjoyable response to the living world. There are the physical effects: sleeplessness, feeling as listless as a zombie, a kind of numbness, loss of strength and energy, but more particularly, an odd fragility, along with a fidgety restlessness. There is also the loss of pleasure: Food, like everything else within the scope of sensation, is without savour. Then there is the vanishing of hope which takes on a despair so intense it is like physical pain, a pain so unendurable that suicide seems a solution.

Here is how one girl who was encompassed by depression (she was 16 years old when she had it) described it later:

> *"The experience of depression is like falling into a deep, dark hole that you cannot climb out of. You scream as you fall, but it seems like no one hears you. Some days you float upward without really trying; on other days, you wish that you would hit bottom so that you would never fall again. Depression affects the way you interpret events. It influences the way you see yourself and the way you see other people. I remember looking in the mirror and thinking that I was the ugliest creature in the world. Later in life, when some of these ideas would come back, I learned to remind myself that I did not have those thoughts yesterday and chances were that I would not have them tomorrow or the next day. It is like waiting for a change in the weather."*

She also remarks that she was angry, cynical, and in great emotional pain and that she thought of suicide as a solution to her unhappiness. Her increasing preoccupation with her own death at that time was "just exhaustion. I was tired of dealing with the anxiety and depression day in and day out."

What is Sadness?

Depression can be placed on a continuum of severity, from feeling mildly depressed in the morning (something most of us experience once in a while) to feeling so deeply depressed and hopeless that suicide is the only option. In major depression, life is paralysed; no new beginnings emerge. The very symptoms of depression tell of a life on hold. So what of sadness?

My focus here is the far more common sadness that at its upper limits becomes, technically speaking, a "sub-clinical depression" - that is, ordinary melancholy. This is a range of despondency[1] that people can handle on their own, if they have the internal resources. Unfortunately, some of the strategies people often resort to can backfire, leaving them feeling worse than before. One such strategy is staying alone, which is often appealing when people are feeling down; more often than not, however, it only adds a sense of loneliness and isolation to the sadness. That may partly explain why studies have found that the most popular tactic for battling depression is socializing- going out to eat, to watch a sport or movie; in short, doing something with friends or family. That can work well if the net effect is to get the person's mind off his sadness. But it simply prolongs the mood if he uses the occasion just to mull over what put him in the depressed state.

A main function for *sadness* is to help adjust to a significant loss, such as the death of someone close or a major disappointment. Sadness brings a drop in energy and enthusiasm for life's activities, particularly pleasures, and, as it deepens and approaches depression, slows the body's metabolism. This introspective withdrawal creates the opportunity to mourn a loss or a frustrated hope, grasp its consequences for one's life, and, as energy returns, plan new beginnings.

[1] Despondency is a loss of hope, feeling miserable. It is not the same as depression in that despondency tends to be transient

3

and has a more temporary nature, and does not have the
potency of symptoms that depression has.

Rumination

Think back over the last month of your life. It may seem normal in most respects; you may have worked or studied during the week, socialized on the weekend, and thought about the future once in a while. Perhaps you were anticipating with some pleasure the next holiday or seeing old friends. But maybe sometime during the past month you also felt kind of down, because you broke up with your boyfriend/girlfriend or, worse yet, somebody close to you died. Think about your feelings during this period. Were you sad? Perhaps you remember crying. Maybe you felt listless (lethargic), and you couldn't seem to get up the energy to go out with your friends. It may be that you feel this way once in a while for no good reason you can think of, and your friends think you're moody.

If you are like most people, you know your mood will pass. You will be back to your old self in a day or two. In fact, if you *never* felt down and always saw only what was good in a situation, it might be more remarkable than if you were depressed once in a while. Feelings of depression (and joy) are universal, which makes it all the more difficult to understand disorders of mood, disorders so incapacitating that violent suicide may seem by far a better option than living (as in the case of the young teenager mentioned in the previous chapter).

Think for a moment about your own experience of depression. What are the major differentiating factors between your feelings and the kind of major depression described in the first chapter? The young girl's depression in this case was outside the boundaries of normal experience by virtue of its intensity and duration. In addition, her severe or "clinical" depression interfered substantially with her ability to function. Finally, a number of associated psychological and physical symptoms accompany severe depression.

We mentioned in the previous chapter that people may resort to certain tactics in battling depression, but we also said that they may work if the net effect is to get that person's mind off his sadness. It simply prolongs the mood if he uses the occasion just to mull over what put him in the depressed mood. Indeed, one of the main determinants of whether a depressed mood will persist or lift is the degree to which people ruminate. Ruminating (worrying) about what's depressing us, it seems, makes the depression all the more intense and prolonged. In depression, worry takes several forms, all focusing on some aspect of the depression itself - how tired we feel, how little energy or motivation we have, for instance, or how little work we're getting done. Typically, none of this reflection is accompanied by any concrete course of action that might alleviate the problem. Other common worries include isolating yourself and thinking about how terrible you feel, worrying that your spouse might reject you because you are depressed, and wondering whether you are going to have another sleepless night.

You may read more on the aspect of rumination in the following chapter.

Don't Ruminate

Depressed people sometimes justify this kind of rumination (constantly reflecting) by saying they are trying to understand themselves better; in fact they are priming the feelings of sadness without taking any steps that might actually lift their mood. Thus in counselling therapy it might be perfectly helpful to reflect deeply on the causes of a depression, if that leads to insights or actions that will change the conditions that cause it. But a passive immersion in the sadness simply makes it worse.

Rumination can also make the depression stronger by creating conditions that are, well, more depressing. Women are far more prone to ruminate when they are depressed than are men. This may at least partly explain the fact that women are diagnosed with depression twice as often as men. Of course, other factors may come into play, such as women being more open to disclosing their distress or having more in their lives to be depressed about. And men may drown their depression in alcoholism, for which their rate is about twice that of women.

Changing these thought patterns has been found in some studies to be on a par with medication for treating mild depression, and superior to medication in preventing its return. Two strategies are particularly effective in the battle. One is to learn to challenge the thoughts at the centre of rumination- to question their validity and think of more positive alternatives. The other is to schedule pleasant, distracting events.

One reason distraction works is that depressing thoughts are automatic, intruding on one's state of mind unbidden. Even when depressed people try to suppress their depressing thoughts, they often cannot come up with better alternatives; once the depressive tide of thought has started, it has a powerful magnetic effect on the train of association[1]. The tendency for depression to perpetuate itself shades even the kinds of distractions people choose. People who are already depressed need to make a special effort to get their

7

attention on something that is completely upbeat, being careful not to inadvertently choose something- a tearjerker movie, a tragic novel- that will drag their mood down again.

> [1] *Train of association: For example, when a person is depressed, then the tendency is to dwell on things that maintain or even intensify the depressed mood.*

Mood Disorders

The disorders that will be described in the next several chapters used to be categorized under several different labels, such as "depressive disorders," "affective disorders," or even "depressive neuroses." Now, these problems are grouped under the heading **mood disorders** because they are characterized by gross deviations in mood.

The fundamental experiences of depression and mania contribute, either singly or together, to all the mood disorders.

The most commonly diagnosed and most severe depression is called a **major depressive episode.** The criteria typically indicate an extremely depressed mood state that lasts for *at least* two weeks and includes cognitive symptoms (such as feelings of worthlessness and indecisiveness) and disturbed physical functions (such as altered sleeping patterns, significant changes in appetite and weight, or a very notable loss of energy) to the point that even the slightest activity or movement requires an overwhelming effort. The episode is usually accompanied by a marked general loss of interest and of the ability to experience any pleasure from life, including interactions with family or friends and accomplishments at work or school. (The inability to experience pleasure is termed *anhedonia*.) Physical changes (sometimes called somatic symptoms) are often central to this disorder.

The second fundamental state in mood disorders is abnormally exaggerated elation, joy, or euphoria. In **mania,** individuals find extreme pleasure in every activity. They become extraordinarily active (hyperactive), requiring very little sleep, and may develop grandiose plans, believing they can accomplish anything they desire. Speech is typically very rapid and may become incoherent because the individual is attempting to express so many exciting ideas at once; this characteristic is typically referred to as *flight of ideas.* Irritability is often part of a manic episode, usually near the end. Paradoxically, being anxious or depressed is also commonly part of mania, as described later. A manic episode may even last up to 3 to 6 months.

We also have what is called a **hypomanic episode,** a less severe version of a manic episode that does not cause so much disruption in one's social life or work, as does a manic episode. (*Hypo* means "below"; thus the episode is below the level of a manic episode.)

Individuals who experience either depression or mania are said to suffer from what is called a *unipolar mood disorder*, because their mood remains at one 'pole' of the usual depression-mania continuum. Because mania by itself is extremely rare, almost everyone with a unipolar mood disorder suffers from unipolar depression. Someone who alternates between depression and mania is said to have a *bipolar mood disorder,* travelling from one 'pole' of the depression-elation continuum to the other and back again. However, this label is a little misleading, because depression and elation may not exactly be at opposite ends of the same mood state; in fact, though related, they are often relatively independent. An individual can experience manic symptoms but feel somewhat depressed or anxious at the same time. This combination is usually called a **mixed episode.** An individual who has this usually experiences such symptoms of mania as being out of control or dangerous and becomes anxious or depressed about them. Recent research suggests that manic episodes are characterized by dysphoric (anxious or depressive) features more commonly than was once thought and dysphoria can be severe.

The rare individual who suffers from manic episodes alone also falls under the category of bipolar mood disorder because experience shows that this individual can be expected to become depressed at a later time. Depression and mania may differ from one person to another in terms of their severity and the frequency with which they tend to recur.

The most easily recognized mood disorder is **major depressive disorder,** defined by the absence of manic or hypomanic episodes before or during the episode. We now know that an occurrence of just one isolated depressive episode in a lifetime is rare. Clinical scientists have concluded that unipolar depression is almost always a chronic condition that waxes and wanes over time but seldom disappears.

Dysthymic disorder shares many of the symptoms of major depressive disorder but differs in that the symptoms are somewhat milder but remain relatively unchanged over long periods of time, and the number of symptoms is less. In fact, it seems that most people suffering from dysthymia eventually experience a major depressive episode.

Recently, individuals have been studied who suffer from both major depression episodes *and* dysthymic disorder, and who are therefore said to have **double depression.** Typically, dysthymic disorder develops first, perhaps at an early age, and then one ore more major depressive episodes occur later. In one study, it was found that 61% of people suffering from double depression had not recovered from the underlying dysthymic disorder 2 years after the follow-up.

Grief

In a previous chapter I asked if you had ever felt down or depressed. Almost everyone has. But if someone you love has died - particularly if the death was unexpected and the person was a member of your immediate family - you may, after your initial reaction to the trauma, have experienced most of the symptoms of a major depressive episode: anxiety, emotional numbness, and denial. In fact, the frequency of severe depression following the death of a loved one is so high (approximately 62%) that psychologists do not consider it a disorder unless very severe symptoms such as psychotic features or suicidal ideation, or less alarming symptoms last <u>longer</u> than 2 months. Some grieving individuals require immediate treatment because they are so incapacitated by their symptoms (e.g., severe weight loss, no energy whatsoever) that they cannot function.

We must confront death and process it emotionally. All religions and cultures have rituals, such as funerals and burial ceremonies, to help us work through our losses with the support and love of our relatives and friends. Usually the natural grieving process resolves within the first several months, although some people grieve for a year or longer. Grief often recurs at significant anniversaries, such as the birthday of the loved one, holidays, and other meaningful occasions, including the anniversary of the death. Psychologists are concerned when someone does *not* grieve after a death, because <u>grieving is our natural way of confronting loss</u>.

Grief is the emotional numbness, disbelief, separation anxiety, despair, sadness, and loneliness that accompany the loss of someone we love. Grief is not a simple emotional state but rather a complex, evolving process with multiple dimensions. In this view yearning for the lost person is one important dimension. Yearning reflects an intermittent, recurrent wish or need to recover the lost person. Another important dimension of grief is separation anxiety, which not only includes yearning and preoccupation with thoughts of the deceased person but also focuses on places and things associated with the deceased, as well as crying or sighing. Grief may also involve despair and sadness, which include a sense of hopelessness and defeat, depressive symptoms, apathy, loss of meaning for activities that used to involve the person who is gone, and growing desolation.

These feelings do not present a clear-cut stage but occur repeatedly shortly after a loss. As time passes though, yearning and protest over the loss tend to diminish, although episodes of depression and apathy may remain or increase. The sense of separation anxiety and loss may continue to the end of one's life, but most of us emerge from grief's tears, turning our attention once again to productive tasks and regaining a more positive view of life.

The grieving process is more like a roller-coaster ride than an orderly progression of stages with clear-cut time frames. The ups and downs of grief often involve rapidly changing emotions, meeting the challenges of learning new skills, noticing personal weaknesses and limitations, and creating new patterns of behaviour. For most individuals, grief becomes more manageable over time, with fewer abrupt highs and lows. Even though time has brought some healing, many wives/husbands have never gotten over their loss. They have just learned to live with it.

Cognitive (basically, all our mental processes) factors are involved in the severity of grief after a loved one has died. The more negative beliefs and self-blame people have, the more severe the symptoms of traumatic grief, depression, and anxiety become.

Long-term grief is sometimes masked and can predispose individuals to become depressed and even suicidal. Good family communication can help reduce the incidence of depression and suicidal thoughts. For example, in one study, family members who communicated poorly with each other had more negative grief reactions six months later than those who communicated effectively with each other just after the loss of a family member.

When grief lasts beyond the normal time, psychologists become concerned. After a year or so, the chance of recovering from severe grief without treatment is considerably reduced and for a small percentage of them, a normal process becomes a disorder. In this case, normal grief response turns into **pathological grief reaction.** Particularly prominent symptoms include intrusive memories and distressingly strong yearnings for the loved one, and avoiding people or places that are reminders of the loved one. In cases of long-lasting grief, the rituals intended to help us face and accept death were ineffective. As with victims suffering from post-traumatic stress one therapeutic approach is to help grieving individuals re-experience the trauma under close supervision. Usually the grieving person is encouraged to talk about the loved one, the death, and the meaning of the loss while experiencing all the associated emotions, until he or she can come to terms with reality. This would include finding some meaning in the traumatic loss, incorporating positive emotions associated with memories of the relationship into the intense negative emotions connected with the loss, and arriving at the position that one can cope with the pain and life will go on.

Children and Adolescents

You might assume that depression requires some experience with life, that an accumulation of negative events or disappointments might create pessimism, which then leads to depression. Like many reasonable assumptions in psychopathology, this one is not uniformly correct. We now have evidence that 3-month-old babies can become depressed. Infants of depressed mothers display marked depressive behaviours (sad faces, slow movement, lack of responsiveness), even when they interact with a non-depressed adult. Whether this behaviour or temperament is due to a genetic tendency inherited from the mother, or the result of early interaction patterns with a depressed mother or a combination of both is not yet clear.

Most psychology investigators agree that mood disorders (in psychopathology, depression is defined as a mood disorder) are fundamentally similar in children and in adults. However, the 'look' of depression changes with age. For example, children under 3 years of age might manifest depression by their facial expressions as well as by their eating, sleeping, and play behaviour, quite differently from children between the ages of 9 and 12. Depressed adolescents are particularly vulnerable to low self-esteem and self-consciousness, as compared to adolescents with non-depressive disorders. Also, adolescents forced to limit their activities because of illness or injury are at high risk for depression.

Depressive disorders occur *less frequently* in children than in adults but rise dramatically in adolescence where, depression is typically *more frequent* than in adults. Children below the age of 9 who are depressed are typically irritable and have emotional mood swings, and they are often mistaken as being hyperactive. In addition, depressed children's symptoms are more chronic in that they are always present rather than episodic as in adults, and this presentation seems to continue through adolescence. It is also well documented that mild depression can be expressed in children as aggression.

15

Further, adolescent girls consistently have higher rates of depression than adolescent boys. Among the reasons for this gender difference are that:

- Females tend to ruminate in their depressed mood and amplify it.
- Females' self-images, especially their body images, are more negative than males'.
- Females face more discrimination than males do.
- Puberty occurs earlier for girls than for boys, and as a result girls experience a piling up of changes and life experiences in the middle school years, which can increase depression.

Certain family factors place adolescent girls at risk for developing depression. These include having a depressed parent, emotionally unavailable parents, parents who have high marital conflict, and parents with financial problems.

Poor peer (of same age) relationships are also associated with adolescent depression. Not having a close relationship with a best friend, having less contact with friends, and experiencing peer rejection all increase depressive tendencies in adolescents, as does the experience of difficult changes or challenges and parental divorce. Also, going through puberty plays a role in some adolescents.

The average age for the onset of a major depressive disorder is about 25 years, but the average age of onset seems to be decreasing. A disturbing finding is that the incidence of depression seems to be steadily increasing, with recent studies suggesting that this trend toward developing depression at increasingly earlier ages is occurring worldwide.

Children and Adolescents II

As we mentioned in a previous chapter in this book, the length of depressive episodes is variable, with some lasting as little as 2 weeks; in more severe cases, an episode might last for several years, with the average duration of the first episode being 6 to 9 months if untreated. Some severe episodes may even last up to 5 years or longer. Occasionally, however, episodes may not entirely clear up, leaving some residue symptoms. In this case, the likelihood of a subsequent episode is much higher.

Investigators have found a rather high percentage of cases of children with dysthymic disorder (dysthymia is also mentioned in a previous chapter in this book). What has also been discovered by one study is that 76% of a sample of dysthymic (low spirits) children later developed major depressive disorder.

Dysthymic disorder may last 20 to 30 years or more, although the average is about 5 years in adults and 4 years in children. Dysthymia has a strong chronicity, that is, it can last a long time. Most children with dysthymia eventually recover from it. It is relatively common for major depressive episodes and dysthymic disorder to co-occur (double depression). Among those who have had dysthymia, as many as 79% have also had a major depressive episode at some point in their lives.

We mentioned earlier that depression in adolescence is higher in girls than it is in boys and we mentioned a few reasons as to why this could be. Depression in adolescent girls also has many manifestations; it tends to make them sluggish/apathetic, yet others, angry and hate filled; some girls even resort to anorexia, bulimia, or carving on their bodies; some withdraw deep within themselves and some even swallow pills; others drink heavily or are promiscuous. Whatever the outward manifestation of the depression, the *underlying* reason is sometimes the grieving for the lost true self, the authentic adolescent girl who disappeared with adolescence. Some are depressed because they feel that they are

17

almost forced to abandon and betray their loving/warm family bonds in order to fit into peer culture.

Self-mutilation can be described as psychic pain turned inward in the most physical manner; it may be an act of protest, a cry for help, or indeed an effort to regain control.

Eating Disorders

Young women come of age in a culture that is obsessed with thinness, especially thinness in women. Eating disorders are not normal; in many cases they arise from distorted eating behaviours that are rooted in *excessive* dieting or the pursuit of unrealistic standards of thinness. The major types of eating disorders are **anorexia nervosa** and **bulimia nervosa.**

Most of the time, eating disorders develop in women during adolescence and young adulthood when social pressures to conform to an unrealistically thin ideal are at their peak. Women with eating disorders outnumber men with eating disorders by at least 6 to 1. The incidences of anorexia nervosa and bulimia nervosa have increased markedly in recent years. Not only are eating disorders disturbing and dangerous in themselves, but they also frequently set the stage for severe depression.

Anorexia nervosa is a potentially life-threatening psychological disorder characterized by maintenance of an abnormally low body weight (refusal to maintain a healthy body weight), intense fear of gaining weight and being overweight, a distorted body image, and in women, lack of menstruation (monthly period).

Women with anorexia may lose 25% or more of their body weight in a year. Severe weight loss stops ovulation. Their overall health declines. Overall, the most deaths are caused by emaciation (being thin and weak) or suicide.

As many as 1% of young women suffer from anorexia. In the typical pattern, a girl notices some weight gain after menarche (a girl's first menstrual period) and decides that it must come off. However, dieting - and, often, exercise - continue at a fever pitch. They persist even after the girl reaches an average weight, and even after family members and others have told her that she is losing too much weight. Girls with anorexia almost always adamantly deny that they are wasting away. They may point to their extreme

19

exercise program as proof of their fitness. But their body images are distorted. Others may perceive them as "skin and bones." But the women themselves frequently sit before the mirror and see themselves as still having pockets of fat.

Many people with anorexia become obsessed with food. They engross themselves in cook books, take on the family shopping chores, and prepare elaborate dinners- for others.

Maria begins the day by eating eggs and toast. Then she binges on cookies; doughnuts; cakes smothered in butter, cream cheese, and jelly; chocolate bars; and bowls of cereal and milk- all within 45 minutes. When she cannot take in any more food, she turns her attention to purging. She goes to the bathroom, ties back her hair, turns the shower on to mask any noise she will make, drinks a glass of water, and makes herself vomit. Afterwards she vows, "Starting tomorrow, I'm going to change." But she knows that tomorrow she will probably do the same thing. [Adapted from a real case with a changed name]

Maria's problem, bulimia nervosa, is characterized by recurrent cycles of binge eating followed by dramatic measures to purge the food. Binge eating often follows food deprivation- for example, severe dieting. Purging includes self-induced vomiting, fasting or strict dieting, use of laxatives, and/or vigorous exercise. Like young women with anorexia, those with bulimia tend to hold perfectionist views about body shape and weight, and express unhappiness with their own body shape. But unlike women with anorexia, those with bulimia generally maintain a relatively normal weight level.

The underlying causes of eating disorders are complex and involve a multitude of factors, for example, a preoccupation with thinness, social pressure to conform to a thin ideal. One of the key factors though, which has recently been given much attention is emotional deficits, particularly a failure to tell distressing feelings from one another and to control them. In one study carried out in a high school it was found that even by 13 years old, there were 61 girls who already had serious symptoms of anorexia or bulimia. The greater the problem, the more the girls reacted to setbacks, difficulties, and minor annoyances with intense negative feelings that they could not soothe, and the lesser the awareness of what, exactly, they were feeling. When these two emotional tendencies were coupled with being highly dissatisfied with their body, then the outcome was anorexia or bulimia. Overly controlling parents have been found not to play a prime role in causing eating disorders, although parents can become intensely controlling *in response* to their daughter's eating disorder, out of desperation to help her.

Eating Disorders II

Some obese people are unable to tell the difference between being scared, angry, and hungry, and so lump all those feelings together as signifying hunger, which leads them to overeat whenever they feel upset. In one study on young girls and eating disorders, it was found that those girls had poor awareness of their feelings and body signals; that was the strongest single predictor that they would go on to develop an eating disorder within the next two years. Most children learn to distinguish among their sensations; to tell if they're feeling bored, angry, depressed, or hungry- it's a basic part of emotional learning. But girls with eating disorders typically have trouble distinguishing among their most basic feelings. They may have a problem with their boyfriend, and not be sure whether they're angry, or anxious, or depressed- they just experience an emotional storm that they do not know how to deal with effectively. Instead they learn to make themselves feel better by eating; this can become a strongly entrenched habit.

But when this habit for soothing themselves interacts with the pressures girls feel to stay thin, the way is paved for eating disorders to develop. At first a girl might start with binge eating. But to stay thin she may turn to vomiting or laxatives, or intense physical exertion to undo the weight gain from overeating. Another avenue this struggle to handle emotional confusion can take is for a girl not to eat at all- it can be a way to feel she has at least some control over such overwhelming feelings.

The combination of poor awareness and weak social skills means that these girls, when upset by friends or parents, fail to act effectively to soothe either the relationship or their own distress. Instead, their upset triggers the eating disorder, whether it be that of bulimia or anorexia, or simply binge eating. Effective treatment for such girls needs to include some remedial instruction in the emotional skills they lack. Psychologists know that if those deficits are addressed, therapy works better. Such girls need to learn to identify their feelings and learn ways to soothe themselves or handle their relationships better, without turning to their maladaptive eating habits to do the job.

Girls are growing up in a society preoccupied with unnatural thinness as a sign of female beauty. Girls with average or heavier-than-average figures feel more pressure to slim down. Well in advance of adolescence, girls are already self-conscious about their weight. Investigators find that even in children as young as eight, disproportionately more girls are dissatisfied with their bodies as boys.

Biological factors are also implicated by findings that anorexia and bulimia tend to run in families. Furthermore, researchers have uncovered evidence pointing to genetic factors involving obsessionistic and perfectionist personality styles as increasing the risk of these disorders. Anorexia is frequently found together with depression, and perhaps the two disorders - anorexia nervosa and depression - share genetic as well as environmental* factors. One theory points to genetic factors which create a vulnerability to eating disorders, and cultural and familial emphasis on body shape and personal perfectibility contribute to the likelihood of developing anorexia, bulimia, and depression.

Men, like women, are under social pressure to conform to an ideal body image- one that builds their upper bodies and trims their abdomens. Gay males tend to be more concerned about their body shape than heterosexual males, and are therefore more vulnerable to eating disorders.

* The term environment in this context does not mean the natural environment around us as such, i.e. sky, trees, buildings etc. In psychology the term environment refers to every non-genetic influence, from prenatal (the period before giving birth) nutrition to the people and situations around us.

Prevention in Children

Particularly in young people, problems in relationships are a trigger for depression. In children the difficulty is as often with their peers as it is with their parents. Depressed children and teenagers are frequently unable or unwilling to talk about their sadness. They seem unable to label their feelings accurately, showing instead a sullen irritability, impatience, crankiness, and anger- especially toward their parents. This, in turn makes it harder for their parents to offer the emotional support and guidance the depressed child actually needs, setting in motion a downward spiral that typically ends in constant arguments and alienation.

A new look at the causes of depression pinpoints deficits in two areas of emotional competence: relationship skills, on the one hand, and a *depression-promoting* way of interpreting setbacks, on the other. While some of the tendency for depression is genetic, some of that tendency seems due to pessimistic habits of thought that predispose children to react to life's small defeats - a bad grade, arguments with parents, a social rejection - by becoming depressed. And there is evidence to suggest that the predisposition to depression, whatever its basis, is becoming ever more widespread among the young.

This millennium is ushering in an age of melancholy, just as the twentieth century became an age of anxiety. International data shows what seems to be a modern epidemic of depression, one that is spreading side by side with the adoption throughout the world of modern ways. These episodes of depression are beginning at earlier and earlier ages. Childhood depression, once virtually unknown (or, at least, unrecognised) is emerging as a fixture in modern life.

Although the likelihood of becoming depressed rises with age, the greatest increases are among young people. This lowering into childhood of the age when people first experience depression also seems to hold worldwide. As to why this is, some psychologists speculate that there has been a tremendous erosion of the nuclear

24

(immediate) family- a doubling of the divorce rate, a drop in parents' time available to children, and an increase in mobility. The losses of these stable sources of self-identification mean a greater vulnerability to depression.

Others point to the fact that in the last few decades there has been an ascendancy in individualism and a fading of larger beliefs in religion, and in supports from the community and extended family. This means a loss of resources that can buffer you against setbacks and failures. Furthermore, to the extent you see a failure as something that is lasting, and which you magnify to taint everything in your life, you are prone to let a momentary defeat become a lasting source of hopelessness. But if you have a larger perspective, like a belief in God and an afterlife, and you lose your job, it's just a temporary defeat in the grand scheme of things.

That depression should not just be treated, but *prevented,* in children is clear from an alarming discovery: even mild episodes of depression in a child can bode for more severe episodes later in life. This challenges the old assumption that depression in childhood does not matter in the long run, since children supposedly "grow out of it." Of course, every child gets sad from time to time; childhood and adolescence are, like adulthood, times of occasional disappointments and losses large and small with the accompanying grief. The need for prevention is not for those times, but for children for whom sadness spirals downward into a gloom that leaves them despairing, irritable and withdrawn- a far worse melancholy.

The cost to children goes beyond the suffering caused by depression itself. Children learn social skills in their peer relations- for example, what to do if you want something and aren't getting it, seeing how other children handle the situation and then trying it yourself. But being depressed, they are likely to be among the neglected children in school, the ones the other kids don't play with much.

The glumness or sadness such children feel leads them to avoid initiating social contacts, or to look away when another child is trying to engage them- a social signal the other child takes as a rebuff; the end result is that depressed children end up rejected or neglected on the playground. This gap in their interpersonal experience means they miss out on what they would normally learn in the rough-and-tumble of play, and so can leave them social and emotional novices, lagging behind with much catching up to do after the depression lifts. Indeed, when depressed children have been compared to those without depression, they have been found to be more socially inept, to have fewer friends, to be less preferred than others as playmates, to be less liked, and have more troubled relationships with other children.

Another cost to these children is doing poorly in school; depression interferes with memory and concentration, making it harder to pay attention in class and retain what is taught. A child who feels no joy in anything will find it hard to marshal the energy to master challenging lessons. What is heart wrenching, is, if a child is already feeling depressed, and starts doing badly in school, and sits at home by himself instead of playing with other kids.

Prevention in Children II

Just as with adults, pessimistic ways of interpreting life's defeats seem to feed the sense of helplessness and hopelessness at the heart of children's depression. That people who are *already* depressed think in these ways has long been known. What has been recently discovered though, is that children who are most prone to melancholy tend toward this pessimistic outlook *before* they become depressed. This insight suggests a window of opportunity for inoculating them against depression before it strikes.

One piece of evidence comes from studies of children's beliefs about their own ability to control what happens in their lives- for example, being able to change things for the better. This is assessed by children's ratings of themselves in terms such as "When I have problems at home I'm better than most kids at helping to solve the problems" and "When I work hard I get good grades." Children who say none of these positive descriptions have little sense that they can do anything to change things; this sense of helplessness is highest in those children who are most depressed.

As we all remember, report cards are one of the greatest sources of elation and despair in childhood. There is a marked consequence in how children evaluate their role when they get a worse grade than they expected. Those who see a bad grade as due to some personal flaw ("I'm stupid") feel more depressed than those who explain it away in terms of something they could change ("if I work harder, I'll get a better grade).

One study followed children who were rejected by classmates, and tracked which ones continued to be social outcasts the following year. How the children explained the rejection to themselves seemed crucial to whether they became depressed. Those who saw their rejection as due to some flaw in themselves grew more depressed. But the optimists, who felt that they could do something to change things for the better, were not especially depressed despite the continuing rejection. What was also found was, as

27

children progressed through school, those who had the pessimistic attitude had responded to hassles at school and to any additional stress at home by becoming depressed.

The experience of depression itself seems to reinforce pessimistic ways of thinking, so that even after depression lifts, the child is left with what amounts to an emotional scar, a set of convictions fed by the depression and solidified in the mind: that he can't do well in school, is not liked, and that he can do nothing to escape his own brooding moods. These fixed ideas can make the child all the more vulnerable to another depression down the road.

The good news: teaching children more productive ways of looking at their difficulties lowers their risk of depression. In several studies carried out in schools, about one in four students had what psychologists call "low-level depression," that is, not severe enough to say it was beyond ordinary unhappiness as yet. Some may have been in the early weeks or months of what was to become a depression.

These students were helped - in special classes - to learn to challenge the thinking patterns associated with depression, to become more adept at making friends, to get along better with their parents, and to engage in more social activities they found pleasant. They also learned some basic emotional skills, including handling disagreements, thinking before acting, and, perhaps most important, challenging the pessimistic beliefs associated with depression- for example, resolving to study harder after doing poorly on an exam instead of thinking, "I'm just not smart enough."

What a child learns in these classes is that moods like anxiety, sadness, and anger don't just descend on you without your having any control over them, but that <u>you change the way you feel by the way you think</u>. Because disputing the depressing thoughts vanquishes the gathering mood of gloom, it's an instant reinforcer[1] that becomes a habit.

Learning these emotional skills early in adolescence is especially helpful. As one psychologist involved in the studies pointed out, "these children seem to be better at handling the routine teenage agonies of rejection. They seem to have learned this at a crucial window for risk of depression, just as they enter the teenage years. And the lesson seems to persist and grow a bit stronger over the course of the years after they learn it, suggesting that the kids are using it in their day-to-day lives."

The studies underline the fact that even in children with a vulnerability/diathesis for depression, thought patterns play a catalytic role in actually developing depression one the one hand, and, maintaining the depression once it comes. Therefore helping children in their thought patterns is pivotal in inoculating them against the problems of teenage hood and beyond.

1 Reinforcement, in psychology, is basically any event that increases the frequency of certain behaviour. For example, in the case of a child who gets a grade A in class and gets his teacher's praise and the smiles of his classmates, then his effort will be reinforced.

Powerful Antidote

You already know from your own experience the basic difference between optimists and pessimists. Put simply, optimists are people who expect good things to happen to them; pessimists are people who expect bad things to happen to them. People with an optimistic explanatory style tend to be healthier than are people with a pessimistic explanatory style. Pessimists tend to believe that their actions are of little consequence.

Optimism, like hope, means having a strong expectation that, in general things will turn out all right in life, despite setbacks and frustrations. Optimism is an attitude that buffers people against falling into apathy, hopelessness, or depression in the face of tough going. And, as with hope, its near cousin, optimism pays dividends in life (providing of course, it is a realistic optimism; a too-naïve optimism can be disastrous).

We may define optimism in terms of how people explain to themselves their successes and failures. People who are optimistic see a failure as due to something that can be changed so that they can succeed next time around, while pessimists take the blame for failure, ascribing it to some lasting characteristic they are helpless to change. These differing explanations have profound implications for how people respond to life. For example, in reaction to a disappointment such as being turned down for a job, optimists tend to respond actively and hopefully, by formulating a plan of action, say, or seeking out help and advice; they see the setback as something that can be remedied. Pessimists by contrast, react to such setbacks by assuming there is nothing they can do to make things go better the next time, and so do nothing about the problem; they see the setback as due to some personal deficit that will always plague them.

Just why optimism makes such a difference lies in the fact that optimists, by seeing not themselves but something in the situation as the reason for their failures, can change their approach for the next time. While the pessimist's mental set leads to despair, the optimist's spawns hope.

One source of a positive or negative outlook may well be our inborn temperament; some people by nature tend one way or another. But, temperament can be tempered by experience. Optimism and hope - like helplessness and despair - can be learned. Underlying both is an outlook psychologists call *self-efficacy*, the belief that one has mastery over the events of one's life and can meet challenges as they come up. Developing a competency of any kind strengthens the sense of self-efficacy, making a person more willing to take risks and seek out more demanding challenges. And overcoming those challenges in turn increases the sense of self-efficacy. This attitude makes people more likely to make the best use of whatever skills they may have- or to do what it takes to develop them. People's beliefs about their abilities have a profound effect on those abilities. Ability is not a fixed property; there is a huge variability in how one performs. People who have a sense of self-efficacy bounce back from failures; they tend to approach things in terms of how to handle them rather than worrying about what can go wrong.

Like its near cousin optimism, hope has healing power. People who have a great deal of hopefulness are, understandably, better able to bear trying circumstances, including medical difficulties. In a study of people paralysed from spinal injuries, those who had more hope were able to gain greater levels of physical mobility compared to other patients with similar degrees of injury, but who felt less hopeful. Hope is especially telling in paralysis from spinal injury, since this medical tragedy typically involves a man who is paralysed in his twenties by an accident and will remain so for the rest of his life. How he reacts emotionally will have broad consequences for the degree to which he will make efforts that might bring him greater physical and social functioning.

Just why an optimistic or pessimistic outlook should have health consequences is open to any of several explanations. One theory proposes that pessimism leads to depression, which in turn interferes with the resistance of the immune system to tumours and infection. Or it may be that pessimists neglect themselves- some studies have found that pessimists smoke and drink more, and exercise less, than optimists, and are generally much more careless about their health habits. Or it may one day turn out that the physiology of hopefulness is itself somehow helpful biologically to the body's fight against disease.

Having said this, research has shown that stressful life experiences can affect one's level of optimism. Thus, even those individuals who possess a strong optimistic explanatory style may have their optimistic outlook dampened by either continuous stress or extremely stressful life experiences.

In the next chapter we will examine what psychologists call *learned helplessness* which is related to what we have discussed here on optimism and pessimism.

Helplessness

In the previous chapter we briefly talked about optimism and pessimism and its role in depression. Learned helplessness is another concept which influences depression.

The development of a sense of hopelessness is a crucial cause of many forms of depression. People make what is called **attributions**; characteristic ways in which people explain their failures and shortcomings to themselves. The attributions people make are important to the extent that the attributions contribute to a sense of hopelessness. Both anxious and depressed individuals feel helpless and believe they lack control, but only in depression do they give up and become hopeless about ever regaining control. **Learned helplessness** is a theory of depression based on an experiment conducted on dogs. Psychologists exposed dogs to an inescapable electric shock. The dogs learned that they were helpless to escape the shock. Later, a barrier to a safe compartment was removed, offering the animals a way out. But when the dogs were shocked again, they made no effort to escape. Their helplessness, it seems, prevented them from attempting to escape. The lethargy and lack of motivation they displayed resembled that seen in people who are depressed. In humans, the failure to obtain reinforcements for one's efforts - to continually try but fail - can also produce the lethargy and sense of helplessness that was observed in the dogs.

Learned helplessness, results from our perception that we have no control over our environment. An optimistic explanatory style can prevent learned helplessness; a pessimistic style spreads helplessness to all facets of life and can lead to physical illness and depression. Pessimists, make personal, permanent, and persistent explanations to themselves about negative events. Thus, helplessness changes from brief and localized (a specific reason) to long lasting and generalized.

In the beginning of this chapter we mentioned attributions and the role they can play in helplessness and hopelessness. There are specific attributions that we may make and this is called the **attribution model of learned helplessness** which involves attributing a failure to some cause.

These personal styles of explanation, or attributional styles, can be illustrated using the example of having a date that does not work out. An *internal* attribution involves self-blame, as in "I really loused it up." An *external* attribution places the blame elsewhere (as in "Some couples just don't have the right chemistry with each other," or, "She didn't share my beliefs"). A *stable* attribution ("it's my personality") suggests a problem cannot be changed. An *unstable* attribution ("It was because I had a head cold") suggests a temporary condition. A *global* attribution of failure ("I have no idea what to do when I'm with other people") suggests that the problem is quite large. A *specific* attribution ("I have problems making small talk at the beginning of a relationship") chops the problem down to a manageable size.

Pessimists, as well as the depressed, attribute the causes of their failures to internal, stable, and global factors- factors that, in their belief, they are relatively powerless to change.

On the other hand, optimists attribute their failures to external, unstable, and specific causes. Optimists tend to live longer, enjoy better health, and experience less stress and depression than do pessimists. Although learned helplessness can occur at any age, infants and children are particularly vulnerable. Infants learn that a correspondence exists between their responses and outcomes when the responses bring changes in their environment; they learn helplessness when these responses do not bring about desired changes. Major causes of learned helplessness are maternal deprivation and an environment that provides a low level of stimulation and feedback.

The ability to influence outcomes makes them predictable. Predictability enables adaptive preparedness. But, inability to exert influence over things that negatively affect one's life breeds apprehension, apathy, or despair. We mentioned the term *self-efficacy* in other chapters which, if you recall, basically means the 'power of believing you can.' People low in self-efficacy feel helpless, unable to exercise control over life events. They believe any effort is futile. When they encounter obstacles, they quickly give up if their initial attempt to deal with the problem is ineffective. People who are extremely low in self efficacy will not even attempt to cope because they are convinced that nothing they do will make a difference (remember the *stable* attribution discussed earlier). Low self-efficacy can destroy motivation, lower aspirations, interfere with cognitive abilities, and adversely affect physical health.

People high in self-efficacy believe they can deal effectively with events and situations. Because they expect to succeed in overcoming obstacles, they persevere at tasks and often perform at a high level. These people have greater confidence in their abilities than do persons low in self-efficacy, and they express little self-doubt. They also view difficulties as challenges instead of threats. High self-efficacy reduces fear of failure, raises aspirations, and improves problem solving and analytical thinking abilities.

Negative Cognition

Cognitive (cognition basically means our thought processes) psychologists believe that the way we interpret negative life events leads to emotional disorders such as depression. They argue that people who are prone to depression tend to see the world through a kind of darkened mental filter that slants or biases how they interpret life experiences. Minor disappointments become blown out of proportion. They come to expect the worst and tend to focus only on the negative aspects of events. These faulty thinking patterns are called "cognitive distortions" which pave the way for depression in the face of negative life events.

The following are types of cognitive distortions and a description of them:

TYPE OF COGNITVE DISTORTION	DESCRIPTION
All-or-Nothing Thinking	Viewing events in black-or-white terms, as either all good or all bad
Misplaced Blame	Tendency to blame or criticize yourself for disappointments or setbacks while ignoring external circumstances
Misfortune Telling	Tendency to think that one disappointment will inevitably lead to another
Negative Focusing	Focuses your attention only on the negative aspects of your experiences
Dismissing the Positives	Snatching defeat from the jaws of victory by trivializing or denying your accomplishments; minimizing your strengths or assets
Jumping to Conclusions	Drawing a conclusion that is not Supported by the facts at hand
Catastrophizing	Exaggerating the importance of negative events or personal flaws (making mountains out of molehills)
Emotion-Based Reasoning	Reasoning based on your emotions rather than on a clear-headed evaluation of the available evidence
Shouldisms	Placing unrealistic demands on yourself that you "should" or "must" accomplish certain tasks or reach certain goals
Name Calling	Attaching negative labels to oneself or others as a way of explaining your own or someone's behaviour
Mistaken Responsibility	Assuming that you are the cause of other people's problems

Some examples of 'cognitive distortions'(or 'irrational thoughts') are: Does your mind automatically run to the worst possible scenario? (Catastrophizing), if you feel a passing tightness in your chest, do you assume that it must be a sign of heart trouble? (Jumping to Conclusions), do you think that people fail to meet your needs because they are selfish? (Name Calling).These are just a few examples of cognitive distortions.

But, it doesn't have to be like this; there are alternative rational thoughts that challenge irrational, depressing thoughts. For example, in the case of Catastrophizing one may rationalize by saying "This is pretty bad, but it's not the end of the world." Or in the case of Misplaced Blame and Name Calling, one may say "I did something I regret, but that doesn't make me evil or worthless as a person.

Some people slide into depression for no obvious reason even when life has been going well. Often however, biological factors accompany psychological reactions to experience. The mind's negative thoughts somehow influence biochemical events that in a vicious cycle, amplify depressing thoughts.

Recent research reveals how *self-defeating beliefs* (our beliefs are also part of our cognition as well as thoughts) feed the vicious cycle. Depressed people view life through dark glasses. Their intensely negative assumptions about themselves, their situations, and their futures lead them to magnify bad experiences and minimize good ones.

Bipolar Disorders

The main feature of *bipolar disorders* is the tendency to alternate between mania and major depression in an unending roller-coaster ride from the peaks of elation (intense joy) to the depths of despair. Beyond that, bipolar disorders are parallel in many ways to depressive disorders. For example, a manic episode might occur only once or repeatedly. There is also a milder but more chronic version of bipolar disorder called **cyclothymic disorder** which is similar in many ways to dysthymic disorder.

Now, there are two types of bipolar disorders; **bipolar I disorder** and **bipolar II disorder**. In bipolar II disorder, major depressive episodes alternate with hypo-manic episodes, rather than full manic episodes. The criteria for bipolar I are the same, except the individual experiences a full manic episode.

During manic or hypo-manic phases, people often deny they have a problem. Even after going to extremes such as spending extravagant amounts of money or making foolish business decisions, these individuals, particularly if they are in the midst of a full manic episode, are so wrapped up in their enthusiasm and expansiveness that their behaviour seems perfectly reasonable to them. The 'high' during a manic state is so pleasurable; people may stop taking their medication during periods of distress or discouragement in an attempt to bring on a manic state once again.

As we mentioned earlier, *cyclothymic disorder*, like dysthymic disorder, is a chronic alternation of mood elevation and depression that does not reach the severity of manic or major depressive episodes. Individuals with cyclothymic disorder tend to be in one mood state or the other for many years with relatively few periods of neutral mood. This pattern should last for at least 2 years (1 year for children and adolescents) to meet criteria for the disorder. Individuals with cyclothymic disorder alternate between mild depressive symptoms and hypo-manic episodes. In this case, the behaviour is not severe enough to require immediate intervention.

Much of the time, such individuals are just considered moody. However, the chronically fluctuating mood states are, by definition, substantial enough to interfere with functioning. Furthermore, people with cyclothymia should be treated because of their increased risk to develop the more severe bipolar I or bipolar II disorder.

The average age for someone to develop bipolar I is 18, and for bipolar II disorder it is 22, although cases of both can begin in childhood. About one third of the cases of bipolar disorder begin in adolescence, and it is often preceded by minor alternations in mood or, as we mentioned, mild cyclothymic mood swings.

Bipolar Disorders II

It is relatively rare for someone to develop bipolar disorder after the age of 40. Once it does appear, the course is chronic; that is, mania and depression alternate indefinitely.

Typically, cyclothymia is chronic and lifelong. In about one third of patients, cyclothymic mood swings develop into full-blown bipolar disorder. In one study of people with cyclothymia, 60% were female and the age of onset (the beginning of the disorder) was quite young, often during the teenage years or before, with some data suggesting that the most common age was 12 to 14 years. The disorder is often not recognized, and those who suffer from it are thought to be high-strung, explosive, moody, or hyperactive.

Some individuals in the midst of a major depressive or manic episode (remember we said that bipolar disorder is the alternation between the two poles; depression and mania) may experience psychotic symptoms, specifically **hallucinations** (seeing or hearing things that aren't there) and **delusions** (strong beliefs, but inaccurate ones). People with these psychotic features may also have somatic delusions, believing, for example, that their bodies are rotting internally and deteriorating into nothingness. Some may hear voices telling them how evil and sinful they are (*auditory hallucinations*). Such hallucinations and delusions are *called mood congruent* because they seem to be directly related to the depression. On rare occasions, depressed individuals might have other types of hallucinations or delusions such as *delusions of grandeur* (believing, for example, they are supernatural or supremely gifted) that do <u>not</u> seem consistent with the depressed mood. This is a *mood incongruent* (not directly related) hallucination or delusion. Although quite rare, this condition signifies a very serious type of depressive episode that may progress to schizophrenia (or may indeed be a symptom of schizophrenia to begin with). Delusions of grandeur accompanying a manic episode are mood congruent.

Although the above may sound slightly complicated (especially with some of the scientific terms used) the basic concept is understandable: Bipolar disorder has 2 'poles'; the one 'pole' is extreme elation and on the other pole, depression. A person who suffers from this, goes from one pole to the other. The severity of both extremes is what differentiates bipolar I from bipolar II. How often an individual alternates between the 2 poles may vary, but typically those who have bipolar disorder spend much of the time on the depression pole rather than the mania one.

In closing this book, we have seen how sadness and depression are defined, the symptoms, the ways they affect us, the mechanisms involved, how they work within us and what we can do to withstand their affect; everyone according to their strength. Knowing the subtle details and acquiring a little more knowledge about their workings within us can give us those few extra helpful tools and that little bit more competency in dealing with them. I would just like to leave you with an exhortation: For those of you in despair, never lose hope, even if you feel there isn't any. Even if you can't see any- then hope to hope.

Hope is a powerful motivator and by extension a powerful force. Nurture it as best you can. It can hold you while you are collapsing; until the solutions present themselves.

 # Afterword

As we mentioned in the beginning of this book, depression can be placed on a continuum of severity, from feeling mildly depressed in the morning (something most of us experience once in a while) to feeling so deeply depressed and hopeless that suicide is the only option.

The main key to combating depression is to strike at the core of the issues causing it. I must stress again, that ruminating (worrying) about what is depressing us very often makes the depression all the more intense and prolonged. We also noted that in depression, worry takes several forms, all focusing on some aspect of the depression itself - how tired we feel, how little energy or motivation we have, how bad things are, or how little work we're getting done. Typically, none of this reflection is accompanied by any concrete course of action that might alleviate the problem. As we said, changing these thought patterns has been found to be on a par with medication for treating mild depression, and superior to medication in preventing its return.

Remember, changing how we *think* changes how we feel.

I hope you enjoyed this book.

The Psychology and Health series

Stress: We Can Master It.

Depression and Sadness: Never Lose Hope – Even If You Can't See Any.

Drugs and Addictions: Some Things You Might Know, A lot of Things You Might Not.

Body Image: How We See Ourselves and Others; How This Can Lead to Problems.

Know Thyself: The Eternal Struggle of The Heart and Mind.

I Want to Sleep: Why We Struggle to Sleep – How We Can Remedy It.

Diet Better: How Understanding The Psychology Behind Dieting, Can Help You Diet Better and, The Latest Research and Discoveries About The Best Diets.